By Chesteria Dixon

Chesteria's World

By Chesteria Dixon

Chesteria's World

By Chesteria Dixon

Chesteria's World

By Chesteria Dixon

Chesteria's World

Author:

Chesteria Dixon

Editor: Iris M. Williams
Printed in the United States of America.

First Printing, 2017

ISBN-10: 0-9864033-2-6
ISBN-13: 978-0-9864033-2-3

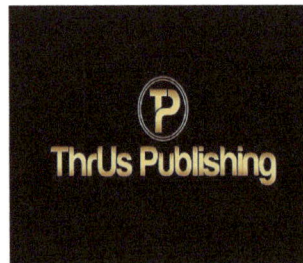

ThrUs Publishing
820 S MacArthur Blvd #105-166
Coppell TX 75019
thruspublishing@hotmail.com

By Chesteria Dixon

Dedication

I would like to dedicate this book to my father (Chester Dixon) and my mother (Nell Dixon) who have filled my world with LOVE,JOY & LOT'S OF LAUGHTER!

"I can do all things through Christ who strengthens me."

Philippians 4:13 KJV

By Chesteria Dixon

My Name is Chesteria,

I'm Daddy's little girl.

By Chesteria Dixon

I'm moma's big helper.

It's all good in my world.

By Chesteria Dixon

I Like ribbons ...

By Chesteria Dixon

... and I like bows.

By Chesteria Dixon

I sing

...and I dance.

By Chesteria Dixon

I Have Lots of Soul!

By Chesteria Dixon

I clean my room...

and make my bed.

By Chesteria Dixon

I don't leave out my clothes, I hang them up instead.

By Chesteria Dixon

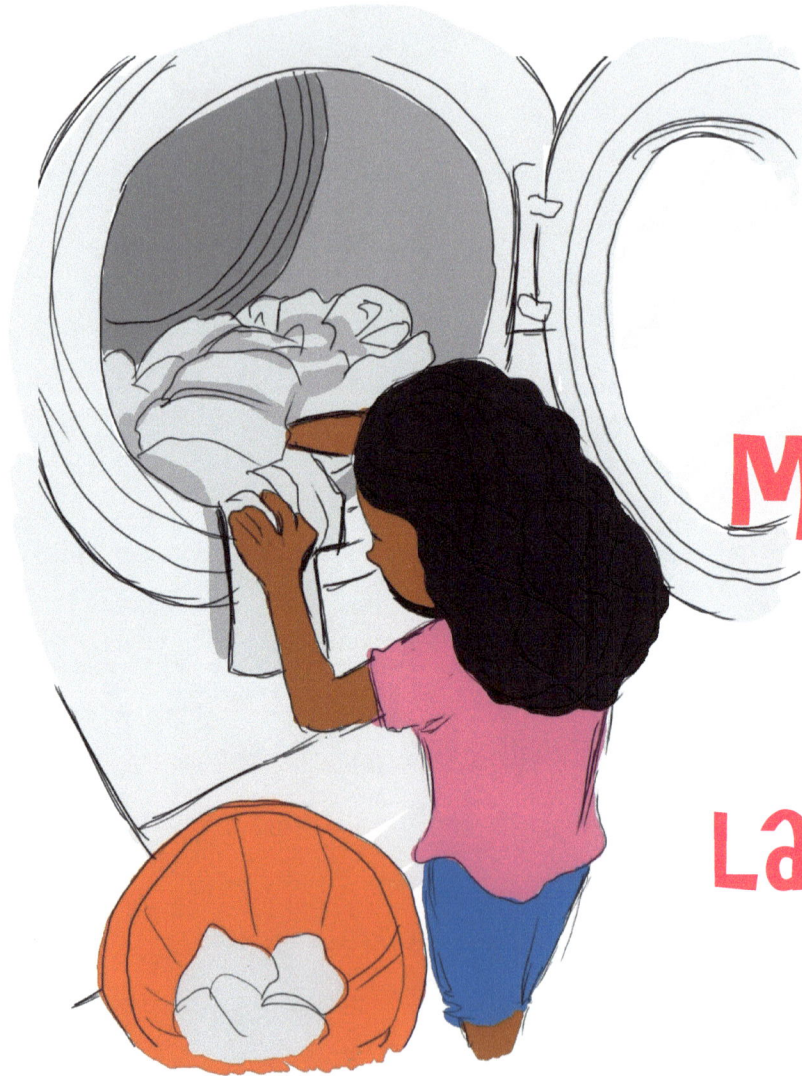

I Help Mommy With Laundry.

By Chesteria Dixon

I even put clothes in the dryer!

Mommy delights

in caring for our family,

By Chesteria Dixon

So
I want to
help
her
with all
the
chores.

I Help Daddy too ...

WHEN HE'S IN THE KITCHEN!

By Chesteria Dixon

I wipe counters, clean dirty dishes,

and lots more that I

could mention.

By Chesteria Dixon

I love going to CHURCH,

to give JESUS WORSHIP and praise!

By Chesteria Dixon

I love the Lord...

It's how I was raised.

By Chesteria Dixon

At School I learn more new things ...

but I get to play too.

That is What Kindergartners do!

By Chesteria Dixon

ONE OF MY HOBBIES IS

LEARNING to act.

Lights
Camera Action

LEARNING LINES IS SERIOUS ... BUT

By CHESTERIA DIXON

It's also lots of fun...

I Listen
For the Words
ACTION!
and
CUT!

By Chesteria Dixon

Family outings are simply the best.

We go to the park and sometimes even to the zoo!

By Chesteria Dixon

We Walk and See the Animals.

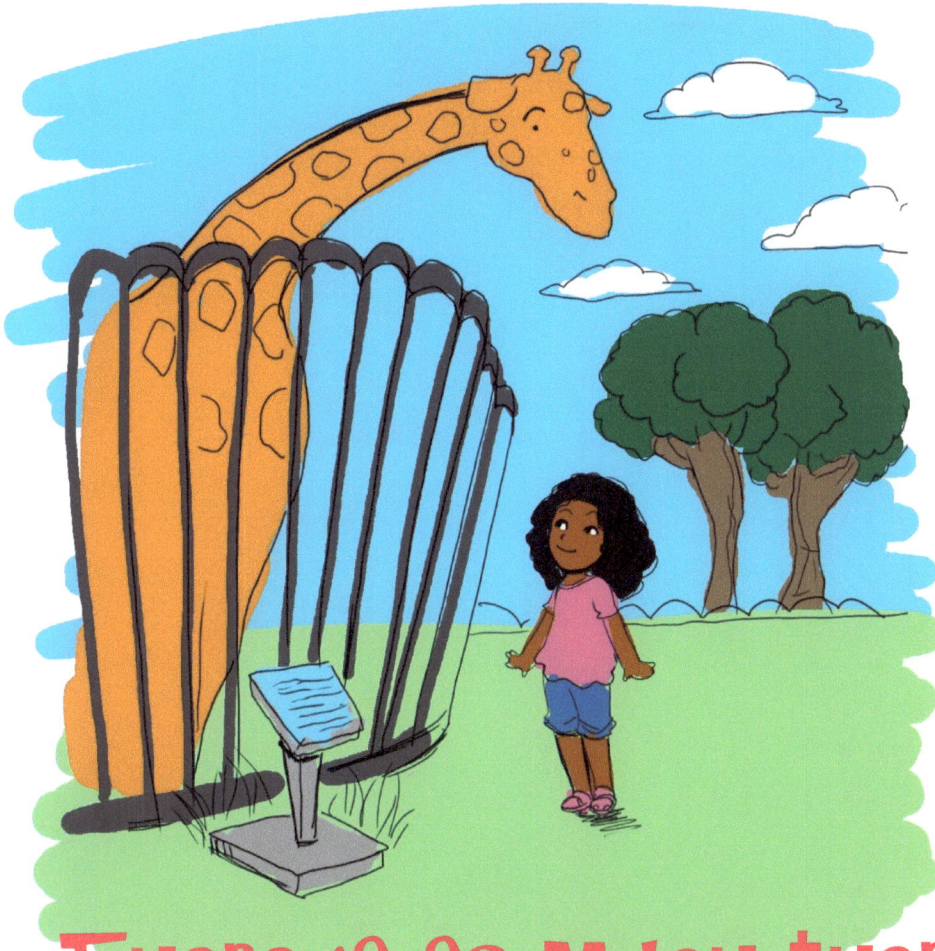

There is so much there that we can do!

By Chesteria Dixon

My name is Chesteria,
and I am an **AWESOME** little girl!
I learn, help, and have fun.
It's all good in *my* world!

By Chesteria Dixon

By Chesteria Dixon

Chesteria's World

By Chesteria Dixon

Chesteria is five years old now,
attends kindergarten
and loves being with her family and friends.

By Chesteria Dixon

Chesteria's World

By Chesteria Dixon

www.ingramcontent.com/pod-product-compliance
Lightning Source LLC
Chambersburg PA
CBHW042103040426
42448CB00002B/116

9 780986 403323